Contents

T0345772

Welcome		2
1 All about school!		4
2 Explore our town!		12
Review Units 1 and 2		20
3 Let's tell stories!		22
4 Party at the library!		30
Review Units 3 and 4		38
5 Let's save our animals!		40
6 Come on an adventure!		48
Review Units 5 and 6		56
Goodbye		58
Celebrations		60
Word connections		62

Welcome to Rise and Shine Library

1 Read and match. Then write.

> reading corner   gallery   courtyard   multimedia room   ~~Biscuit~~

 **1** [d]
 **2** ☐
 **3** ☐
 **4** ☐
 **5** ☐

a *I'm Rafa. I like the r_____ c_____.*

b *I'm Alicia. I like the c_____.*

c *I'm Daniel. I like the g_____.*

d *I'm Thomas. B iscuit_____ is my cat.*

e *I'm Lena. I like the m_____ r_____.*

2 Think and write.

> has   doesn't have

1 The library _____has_____ a multimedia room.

2 The library _____ a bedroom.

3 It _____ a gallery.

4 It _____ an information desk.

5 It _____ a garage.

> **Tell me!**
> Where can you watch movies in the library?

3 Write. Then ask and answer.

Does the library have _____?

Yes, it _____.

Does it have _____?

No, it _____.

> **Extra time?** Do you have a library in your town or school? What does it have?

4 Match. Then listen, circle, and write.

 1
 2
 3
 4

a beanbag

(22) / 32

twenty-two

b computer

13 / 30

_____

c TV

4 / 44

_____

d poster

15 / 50

_____

Let's build!

What does your classroom have?

5 Read and draw.

1

It's four o'clock.

2

It's nine o'clock.

3

It's three-thirty.

4

It's eleven-thirty.

 I can **shine!**

6 Imagine your perfect library. Think and complete.

My perfect library

It has...	It doesn't have...

Extra time? Tell your family about your perfect library.

(3)

All about school!

Let's review! SB p7

Think and write.

25 _twenty_ -five   38 _____ -eight

67 _____ -seven   89 _____ -nine

Lesson 1 ➡ Vocabulary

1 Read and number the pictures.

1 music	2 art	3 English	4 math	5 P.E.
6 history	7 geography	8 technology	9 drama	10 science

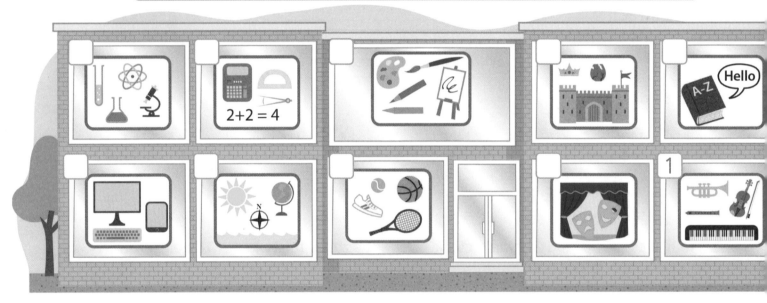

2 Look and write.

1
science

2

3

4

5 Hello

6

7

8

Tell me!
What school subjects use numbers?

4

Extra time? Number the school subjects from 1–10: 1 = ☺ 10 = ☹

1 Listen and circle.

Monday	history	math
Tuesday	art	music
Wednesday	English	geography
Thursday	P.E.	drama
Friday	technology	science

2 Look at Activity 1. Then write.

1 What do you have on Monday?   I have _____math._____

2 What do you have on Tuesday?   I have _____.

3 What _____ you _____ on Wednesday?

I _____.

4 _____ on Thursday?

I _____.

I can shine!

3 Choose a school day. Write the school subjects you have. Then ask and answer.

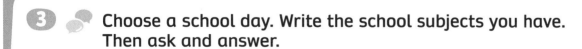

Day: _____   What _____ on _____?

I _____ and _____.

Extra time? Make a flashcard for a difficult word. Draw a picture and write the word.

1 Number for you. Then write.

| brush bed ~~wake~~ breakfast shower school |

I go to _____.

I take a _____.

I go to _____.

I ___*wake*___ up.

I _____ my teeth.

I have _____.

2 SB p12–13 ➡ Read and write true (T) or false (F).

I don't like geography.

I have only 19 teeth, look!

I go to bed at eight o'clock and I wake up at nine o'clock in the morning.

Yes, I think I like math now.

①  F

②

③

④

I can shine!

3 Write for you.

I wake up at _____ on Friday.

I have _____ and _____ on Friday.

I like _____.

Let's imagine!
What do you think?
The story is: OK ☆ good ☆☆ great ☆☆☆

Extra time? What things in your classroom have symmetry? Draw or write.

1 **Look and write.**

1 What time do you wake up? I <u>wake up</u> at <u>seven o'clock.</u>

2 What time _____ you have breakfast?

I _____ at _____.

3 _____ brush your teeth?

_____ at _____.

4 _____ go to bed?

_____

2 **Write. Then number.**

☐ I _____ to school.

☐ How do you _____ to school?

☐ I go to school by _____. And you?

I can shine!

Let's build!
What time do you wake up on Saturday?

3 💬 **Draw and circle. Then ask and answer.**

What time do you wake up?

I wake up at... .

How do you go to school?

Pronunciation Find and circle the one that doesn't belong: boy toy walk

1 Read and match.

1  b

2

Time	Monday	Tuesday	Wednsday	Thursday
9:00	math	technology	art	music
10:00	history	drama	English	math
11:00	science	P.E.	technology	geography
12:00	English	math	science	English

3

4

a This is my classroom. There are twenty students in my class.

b This is the playground. We play after lunch.

c I do my homework at four o'clock.

d This is my school schedule. On Monday, I have math at nine o'clock.

2 🎧 1.17 Listen and check (✓). Then write.

1

a   b ✓

2

a   b

3

a   b

4

a   b

My favorite day is ¹_____Tuesday._____

I have ²_____ on Tuesday.

I play on the ³_____ at lunchtime.

I do my homework at ⁴_____.

All children have the same school day. True or false?

8

1 Read and match.

My school day, by Alex

On school days, I wake up at seven o'clock. [c]

I have breakfast at seven-thirty. ☐

I go to school by bike. ☐

I like Mondays. I have geography, P.E., and drama. ☐

I go to bed at eight-thirty. ☐

(a) (b) (c) (d) (e)

2 Give it a go **Plan your diary entry.**

1 What time do you wake up? _____

2 What time do you have breakfast? _____

3 What time do you go to school? _____

4 What school day do you like? _____

5 What subjects do you have? _____

6 What time do you go to bed? _____

I can shine!

3 Write your diary entry.

My school day, by _____

On school days, I _____ at _____.

I _____.

I _____.

I like _____.

I have _____.

I _____ at _____.

Check your work! Remember to use capital letters! Monday   Friday   English

9

1 **Find and circle. Then write.**

T	E	C	H	N	O	L	O	G	Y
G	W	O	I	Z	T	P	H	Y	M
U	A	R	T	X	T	Z	B	V	U
E	K	B	D	F	P	G	R	O	S
N	E	W	Q	M	E	N	M	L	I
G	U	D	T	L	G	S	D	R	C
L	P	J	H	W	S	P	S	Z	V
I	Y	G	O	T	O	B	E	D	A
S	Y	F	S	D	H	U	I	P	R
H	X	H	I	S	T	O	R	Y	T

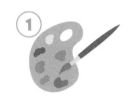 1

 2

art _____

 3

 4

_____   _____

 5

 6
Hello

 7

 8

_____   _____   _____   _____

2 1.20 **Write. Then listen and check (✓).**

 1
Monday   Wednesday
Tuesday   Thursday

What __do__ you __have__ at school on Monday?

I have _____ and _____.

 2

What time do you _____?

I take a shower at _____.

3

What time _____?

I have breakfast _____.

3 💬 **Write and answer for you. Then talk with a friend.**

How do you go to school?   I _____.

Extra time? What are these school subjects? a a d m r e g o g a r y p h h t a m

1 **Think and write.**

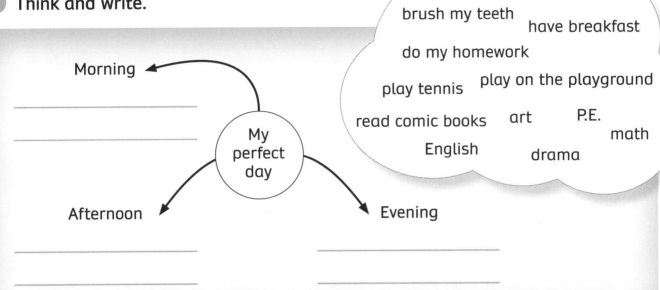

Morning

_____

_____

My perfect day

take a shower

brush my teeth

have breakfast

do my homework

play tennis   play on the playground

read comic books   art   P.E.

English   drama   math

Afternoon

_____

_____

Evening

_____

_____

2 **Make your lapbook. Find pictures or draw. Then write.**

My Perfect Day

1 What time do you wake up? _____

2 How do you go to school? _____

3 What subjects do you have? _____

4 What do you do in the evening? _____

5 What time do you go to bed? _____

My Perfect Day

I wake up at seven o'clock.

I go to school by car.

I love art!

I have art and math.

I go to bed at nine o'clock.

Home-school link 📥 Tell your family about your perfect day.

Explore our town!

Let's review! SB p10–11

Think and write.

What subjects do you have at school today?

_____ _____

_____ _____

Lesson 1 ➡ **Vocabulary**

1 **Read and number.**

| 1 town square | 2 hospital | 3 movie theater | 4 sports center | 5 police station |
| 6 cafe | 7 drugstore | 8 bus stop | 9 grocery store | 10 store |

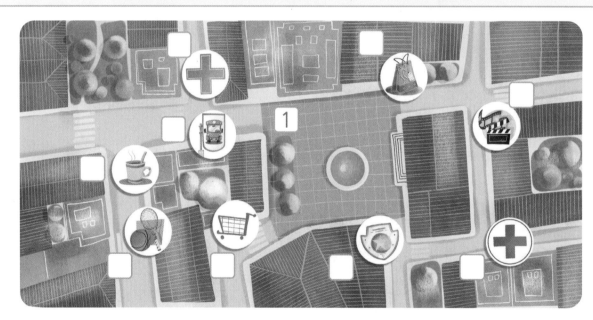

2 **Look and write.**

①

drugstore

②

_____

③

_____

④

_____

⑤

_____

⑥

_____

⑦

_____

⑧

_____

Tell me!
Where can I go when I'm hungry?

Extra time? What places do you go to in your town?

1 🎧 (2.06) **Listen and check (✓) or put an ✗. Then match.**

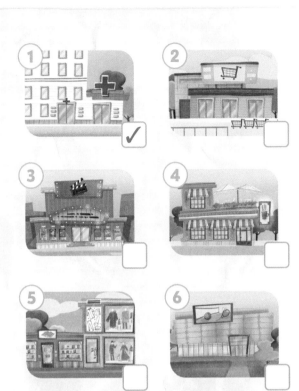

In my town...

1 There's ⟍   a   a grocery store.

2 There's   b   a movie theater.

3 There isn't   c   a hospital.

4 There aren't   d   any cafes.

5 There are   e   a sports center.

6 There isn't   f   some stores.

2 **Look and write.**

> There are some   There aren't any
> ~~There's a~~   There isn't a

1 ___There's a___ drugstore.

2 _____ police station.

3 _____ cafes.

4 _____ bus stops.

I can shine! ✳

3 **Write about your town.**

There's _____ . There isn't _____ .

There are _____ . There aren't _____ .

> **Extra time?** Which new word is difficult for you?

1 Look and write.

doctor   server   librarian   bus driver   sales clerk   police officer

1 ____doctor____

2 _____

3 _____

4 _____

5 _____

6 _____

2 SB p22–23 Read and match.

a **What a great day!**

b **Look! There's the doctor! She's at the bus stop!**

c **There's a bookstore! Let's ask the sales clerk.**

d **Excuse me, officer! This isn't our book.**

I can **shine!**

Let's imagine!
*What do you think?
The story is: OK ☆   good ☆☆
great ☆☆☆*

3 Write for you. Who helps you...

at the library?

_____

at the hospital?

_____

at the stores?

_____

at the police station?

_____

14

Extra time? Is the doctor happy at the end of the story? Why or why not?

1 Look and circle.

1 Is there a police officer?
Yes, there is. / No, there isn't.

2 Is there a bus driver?
Yes, there is. / No, there isn't.

3 Are there any librarians?
Yes, there are. / No, there aren't.

4 Are there any servers?
Yes, there are. / No, there aren't.

2 Order and write. Then say.

> **Let's build!**
> *Is there a bus driver?*
> *Are there any sales clerks?*

live? / you / Where / do
Where _____?

Park / live / I / on / Street.
_____

I can shine! ✳

3 💬 Think and write. Then ask and answer.

Is there a _____ in your town?

Are there any _____?

Where do you _____?

Pronunciation Find and circle the one that doesn't belong: there   park   where

(15)

1 **Read and match.**

① **a**

②

③

④

a I love my community. It's great!

b There's a big fountain in my town square.

c There are some benches.

d People in my town are very friendly.

2 🎧 2.16 **Listen and check (✓). Then write.**

a

b

> cafes   ~~town square~~   community   friendly   movie theater   fountain   stores

This is my ¹ <u>town square</u>. There isn't a ² _____

but there are some ³ _____ and ⁴ _____ .

There's a ⁵ _____ . People in my town are very

⁶ _____ . I love my town and my ⁷ _____ .

What do you like about your community?

Extra time? Say three things you can see in your town square.

1 What is in the sports center? Read and check (✓).

My favorite place, by Maria

My favorite place is the sports center. I play tennis there!

There's a cafe.

It has some nice cookies.

There aren't any stores.

I go there by bus. The bus driver helps me.

I love the sports center!

2 Give it a go **Plan your leaflet.**

1 What's your favorite place in town? _____

2 There's a _____ .

3 There aren't any _____ .

4 Who helps you? _____

I can shine!

3 Write your leaflet.

My favorite place, by _____

There's _____ .

There aren't _____ .

There _____ .

_____ helps me.

_____

Check your work! [.] or [?]: Is there a hospital ☐   There's a hospital ☐

1 Find and circle. Then write.

librarian cafespoliceserversdrugstorestoresmovietheatertownsquare

In my town

There's a...

_____librarian._____

_____

_____

_____

There are some...

_____

_____

_____

_____

2 🎧 2.19 Write. Then listen and check.

Is there a librarian?

No, there _____.

_____ there any servers?

No, there _____.

_____ any doctors?

Yes, _____.

You're at the _____!

3 💬 Write and answer for you. Then talk with a friend.

Where _____ you live?

I _____.

Extra time? You can have breakfast or lunch in this place. It's a... .

1 **Think and write.**

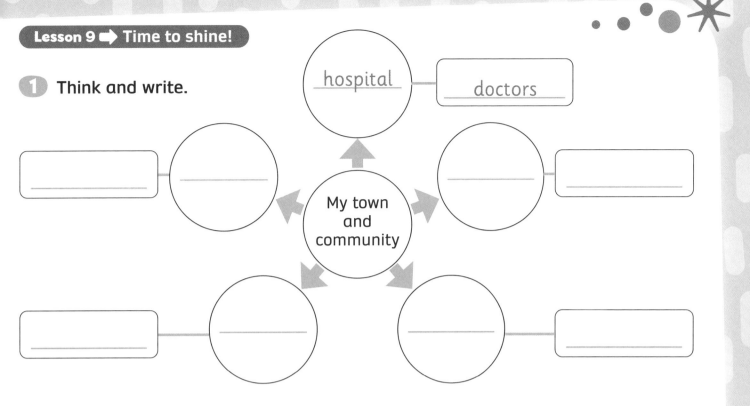

hospital — doctors

My town and community

2 **Make your lapbook. Find pictures or draw. Then write.**

My favorite people and places

1 What places are there in your town? _____

2 What are your favorite places? _____

3 Who helps you? _____

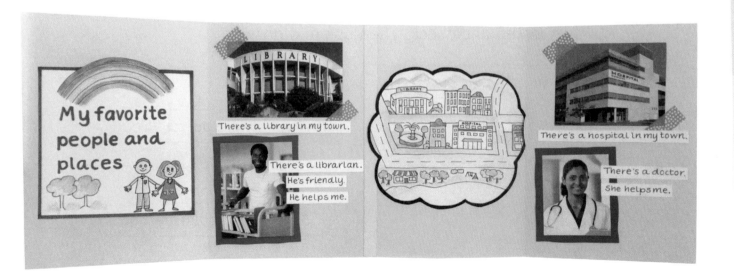

My favorite people and places

There's a library in my town.

There's a librarian. He's friendly. He helps me.

There's a hospital in my town.

There's a doctor. She helps me.

Home-school link Tell your family about your favorite people and places.

19

Review 1 All about us

1 Look, read, and write.

On Saturday, I ¹ _wake up_ at eight-thirty.

I ² _____ at nine o'clock.

I have ³ _____ club at ten-thirty.

After lunch, I go to the ⁴ _____ with my friends.

There are some ⁵ _____ and the ⁶ _____ are very friendly.

I ⁷ _____ at ten o'clock.

2 (2.22) Number. Listen and check. Then ask and answer.

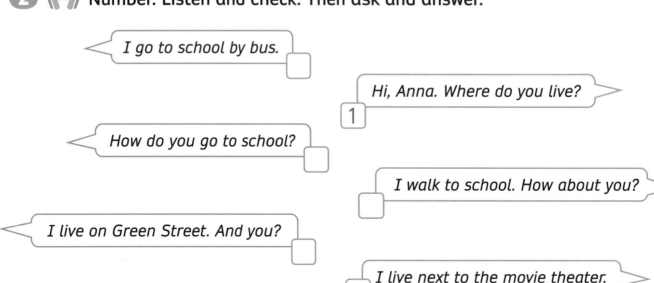

I go to school by bus.

Hi, Anna. Where do you live? [1]

How do you go to school?

I walk to school. How about you?

I live on Green Street. And you?

I live next to the movie theater.

3 Order and write. Then answer for you.

1 breakfast / What / you / time / do / have

<u>What time do you have breakfast?</u>

<u>I have breakfast at   </u>.

2 Friday / What / you / on / do / have

_____?

_____.

3 hospital / there / Is / a / town / your / in

_____?

_____.

4 any / librarians / Are / there / in / town / your

_____?

_____.

Mini-project

4 Think and write.

On Sunday, I _____ .

I have _____ at

_____ .

After lunch, I go to _____ .

There's a _____ .

There aren't any _____ .

_____

Time to shine!

5 Read and check (✓). Tell your friend.

1 I can write a diary entry about my day. ☐

2 I can write a leaflet about my town. ☐

3 I can talk about my daily routine. ☐

4 I can talk about the people and places in my town. ☐

My favorite song is in

Unit 1 ☐   Unit 2 ☐

My favorite story is in

Unit 1 ☐   Unit 2 ☐

6 Vote. Sing or role-play.

Let's tell stories!

Let's review! `SB p20-21`→

Think and write.
Where can you go to...

see a doctor? _____

have lunch? _____

watch a movie? _____

1 **Read and number.**

1 prince	2 superhero	3 spy	4 villain	5 explorer
6 pirate	7 princess	8 astronaut	9 inventor	10 storyteller

2 **Look and write.**

① spy

② _____

③ _____

Tell me!
*He has black hair.
He's tall. He can
fly. Who is he?*

④ _____

⑤ _____

⑥ _____

Extra time? What characters are in your story book?

1 (3.06) Listen and check (✓).

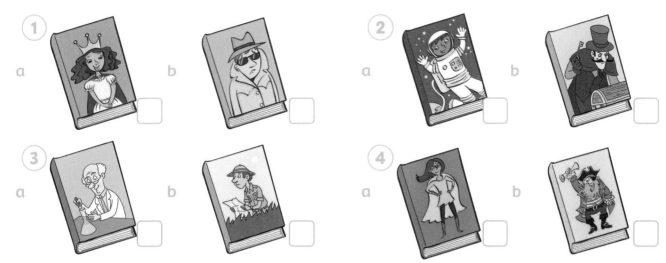

2 Look at Activity 1. Then write.

1
The book is about a ___princess.___

___Is___ she happy?

Yes, she _____.

2
The book is about a _____.

_____ it big?

No, it _____.

3
The book is about a _____.

_____ tall?

Yes, _____.

4
The book is about a _____.

_____ bad?

No, _____.

I can shine!

3 Write about your favorite book.

My favorite book is _____.

It's about _____.

Extra time? Write and spell. pir __ te   sp __   v __ llain   expl __ rer

1 Look and circle. Then write.

cute (strong) scary brave kind smart scary smart

1 The astronaut is ___strong.___

2 The villain is _____.

3 The superhero is _____.

4 The spies are _____.

2 SB p34–35 ➡ Think about the story. Then read and check (✓).

It's about a brother and a sister.
They're scary. ☐

It's about an astronaut. He's cute and smart. ☐

It's about a boy and his friends.
They share their favorite books. ☐

It's about a superhero
and a villain. ☐

Let's imagine!
What do you think?
The story is: OK ☆   good ☆☆
great ☆☆☆

I can shine!

3 Write for you.

My favorite book character is _____.

He's/She's _____.

Extra time? Circle the books you like. I like story / adventure / sticker books.

1 **Look and write.**

1 __Are__ they strong? Yes, they __are.__   3 _____ cute? _____ .

2 _____ they kind? No, they _____ .   4 _____ scary? _____ .

> **Let's build!**
> Ask and answer about superheroes.

2 **Read and circle.**

> I like this book
> about spies.

> I don't like this
> book about pirates.

1 Oh, I do! / So do I!

2 Oh, I do! / So do I!

I can shine!

3 **Write for you. Then talk with a friend.**

> monsters   princesses
> superheroes   villains
> explorers   pirates

> I like books about _____ .
> I don't like books about _____ .

> So do I! / Oh, I do!

Pronunciation Find and circle the one that doesn't belong: brave   boy   very   book

25

1 Read and write true (T) or false (F).

1 Opera tells stories with puppets. [F]

2 Kathak dancers tell stories with dance. The clothes are beautiful. ☐

3 Hula tells stories with dance and chants. It's from Hawaii. ☐

4 Chinese shadow puppets tell stories about princes and princesses. ☐

2 Listen and match. Then write for you.

1 Chinese shadow puppets are   a interesting.
2 Opera is   b fun.
3 Indian Kathak dance is   c beautiful.
4 Hula dancing is   d exciting.

I like __Chinese shadow puppets.__ They're __interesting.__

I like _____ .

*How do you share stories in class?
Do you read books together/
watch movies/make puppets/sing?*

Extra time? At home, we tell stories with... .

1 Read and check (✓).

My movie review, by Theo
I like this movie. It's great! It's about
a superhero and an inventor. They're
brave and strong. There's a spy in
the story, too. He's smart and kind. I think
the movie is very interesting and exciting.

2 Give it a go **Plan your movie review.**

1 It's about _____ and _____.

2 They're _____.

3 There's a _____.

4 He's/She's _____.

5 The movie is fun/interesting/exciting.

I can shine!

3 Write your movie review.

My movie review, by _____

It's _____.

They're _____.

_____

_____

_____

Check your work! Write *a* or *an*: ___ spy ___ astronaut ___ prince ___ villain

27

1 Write the words.

① ② ③ ④ ⑤ ⑥ ⑦ ⑧ ⑨

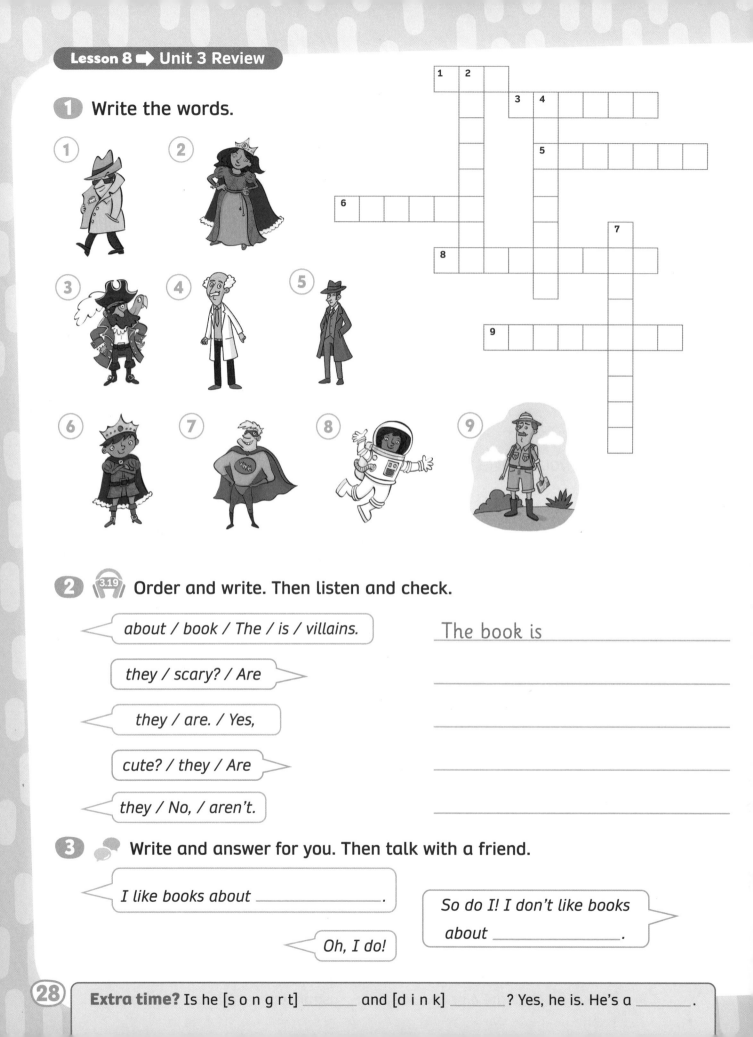

2 (3.19) Order and write. Then listen and check.

about / book / The / is / villains.

The book is _____

they / scary? / Are

_____

they / are. / Yes,

_____

cute? / they / Are

_____

they / No, / aren't.

_____

3 Write and answer for you. Then talk with a friend.

I like books about _____.

So do I! I don't like books about _____.

Oh, I do!

Extra time? Is he [s o n g r t] _____ and [d i n k] _____? Yes, he is. He's a _____.

1 💬 **Think and match. Then talk with a friend.**

prince

princess

explorer

astronaut

pirate

villain

superhero

inventor

cute

strong

scary

brave

kind

smart

tall

small

In my book, the _____
is _____ .

2 **Make your lapbook. Find pictures or draw. Then write.**

My story

1 What's your story about? _____ .

2 Describe the characters. _____ .

3 How can you tell your story? _____ .

Party at the library!

Let's review! SB p32–33

Think and write.

My four favorite book characters are

_____ _____

_____ _____

Lesson 1 ➡ Vocabulary

1 Read and number.

1 playing chess	2 taking pictures	3 coding	4 painting
5 having a party	6 trading cards	7 juggling	8 acting
9 playing video games		10 learning an instrument	

2 Look, read, and write.

1 I have a camera. I like ___taking___ pictures.

2 I like _____ pictures of my friends.

3 It's my birthday. I'm _____ with my family.

4 Drama is my favorite subject. I like _____.

5 I have my violin lesson on Tuesday. I'm _____

_____ .

6 I have three balls. I like _____ .

Tell me!
*I have a computer.
What are my hobbies?*

Extra time? What hobbies can you do with a friend?

1 (4.06) Listen and check (✓) or put an ✗.

	painting	playing chess	trading cards	juggling
James				
Sonia				

2 Look at Activity 1. Then write.

1 James likes _painting._

He likes _____

and _____.

2 He doesn't like _____.

3 Sonia _likes_ _____

and _____.

4 She doesn't _____

and she doesn't _____.

I can shine! ✳

3 Write about your friends.

Alex likes acting. He doesn't like juggling.

☺ _____ likes _____.

☹ _____ doesn't like _____.

☺ _____

☹ _____

Extra time? Order and write. Then draw. coding. / Maria / like / doesn't ⊙⊙

1 Look and write.

being   using   doing
~~helping~~   playing   learning

sports   ~~people~~   outside
something new
crafts   computers

1   _helping people_   2 _____   3 _____

4 _____   5 _____   6 _____

2 SB p44–45 ➡ Read and match.

 ① ☐

 ② ☐

 ③ ☐

 ④ a

a Can I help you learn something new now?

b Wait, where are Lena and Rafa?

c Don't worry, Rafa. I like helping people.

d Does Lena like doing crafts?

I can shine!

Let's imagine!
What do you think?
The story is: OK ☆   good ☆☆
great ☆☆☆

3 Write for you.

Choose your three favorite activities for a party.

I like _____, _____ and _____.

Extra time? Thomas thinks the decorations are... .

1 Order and write. Then answer.

1 like / Does / acting? / he

Does he like acting?

Yes, _he does._

2 she / pictures / taking / Does / like

_____?

No, _____.

3 he / games / like / Does / video / playing

_____

_____?

_____.

4 being / she / like / Does / outside

_____?

_____.

2 Read and number.

Let's build!
Rafa / like / playing sports?

No, I'm not. I want to learn. Are you good at painting?

Yes, I am. Don't worry. You can learn!

OK. Let's go to Art Club!

Are you good at painting?

1

I can shine!

3 💬 Think and write for you. Then talk with a friend. Find two things you both want to learn.

Are you good at _____?

Yes, _____.

OK. Let's go to _____!

No, _____.

Pronunciation Find and circle the one that doesn't belong: singing   thing   learn   coding

1 Read and circle.

1 Origami is Japanese. It means to **(fold)** / **cut** paper.

2 I paint pictures and I **cut** / **knit** them out.

3 Finger knitting is fun! I use my fingers to **stick** / **knit** scarves for my toys.

4 I **fold** / **stick** my favorite pictures in my scrapbook.

2 4.16 Listen and match. Then write.

origami   scrapbooks   knitting

1

I'm good at taking pictures.

a

I'm good at finger _____.

2

I like making scarves for my teddy bears.

b

My favorite craft is _____.

3

I like making paper animals.

c

I like sticking pictures in my _____.

What's a typical craft in your country?

3 Choose a craft you like. Write.

I like doing origami. I fold paper. I make flowers.

_____

Extra time? Which hobbies use paper?
finger knitting   origami   making scrapbooks   coding

1 Read and check (✓). Then circle the instruction words.

_____, by Monty

1 (Fold) a piece of card.

2 Draw a picture of flowers on a piece of paper.

3 Cut out the flowers.

4 Stick your flowers onto the card.

5 Write a message inside.

ⓐ

Make an origami animal

ⓑ

Make a birthday card

2 Give it a go **Choose a different craft. Plan your instructions.**

1 I want to _____.

2 I need _____.

3 Instruction words I can use: _____ _____

_____ _____ _____

4 Step 1: _____.

I can shine!

3 Write your instructions. Then draw.

Make _____, by _____

_____

_____

_____

_____

Check your work! Check your spelling. write knit stick paint

35

1 Unscramble and write.

ginggluj   tacgin   gicodn   aniptgin   glapyin shecs

1 __juggling__   2 _____   3 _____   4 _____   5 _____

iadtnrg darcs   ginbe touedsi   singu persmocut

6 _____   7 _____   8 _____

2 🎧 4.19 Listen and draw. Then write.

① ②

a He ___likes___ playing sports.   a She _____ .

b He _____ learning an instrument.   b She _____ .

c _____ he like playing video   c _____ having a party?

games? _____   _____

3 💬 Order and write. Answer for you. Then talk with a friend.

> *good / taking / Are / at / pictures / you*
>
> _____ ?

> _____

Extra time? It's a craft. You fold paper and you can make animals.
It's _____

1 💬 Think and write. Then talk with a friend.

Hobbies and crafts

Inside   **Both**   **Outside**

_____   _____   _____

_____   _____   _____

2 Make your lapbook. Find pictures or draw. Then write.

My favorite hobbies

1 Hobbies I like: _____

2 I'm good at _____ .

3 outside or inside? _____

4 I do them with _____ .

Home-school link ⬇ Tell your family about your favorite hobbies.

1 **Read and write.**

acting ~~kind~~ chess using smart cards

My best friend is Martin.

He's ¹ ___kind___ and ² _____ .

He's good at ³ _____ computers.

I like swapping ⁴ _____ with Martin.

He likes playing ⁵ _____ .

He doesn't like ⁶ _____ .

2 **(4.22)** **Match. Listen and check. Then ask and answer.**

① Are you good at juggling?

② Are you good at coding?

③ I like stories about pirates.

④ I don't like stories about villains.

ⓐ No, I'm not. But I'm good at painting.

ⓑ Oh, I do!

ⓒ Yes, I am!

ⓓ So do I!

3 Read and circle.

Lily   Tom

1 (Are) / Is they pirates? Yes, they **are** / **aren't**.

2 **Is** / **Are** they cute? No, they **aren't** / **isn't**.

3 **Do** / **Does** Tom like helping people?
Yes, he **does** / **doesn't**.

4 Does Lily **like** / **likes** being outside?
No, she **doesn't** / **do**.

5 **Is** / **Are** Tom scary? Yes, he **is** / **isn't**.

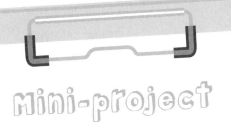

Mini-project

4 Think and write.

My best friend is _____.

He / She's _____.

He / She likes _____.

He / She doesn't like _____.

He / She's good at _____.

I like _____

with _____.

Time to shine!

5 Read and check (✓). Tell your friend.

1 I can write a review about my favorite book. ☐

2 I can write instructions about how to make something. ☐

3 I can talk about books. ☐

4 I can ask and answer about what activities my friends like. ☐

My favorite song is in
Unit 3 ☐   Unit 4 ☐

My favorite story is in
Unit 3 ☐   Unit 4 ☐

6 🎭 Vote. Sing or role-play.

5 Let's save our animals!

Let's review! SB p42–43

Think and write.

Which hobbies can you do outside?

_____ _____

_____ _____

Lesson 1 ➡ Vocabulary

1 Read and number.

1 monkeys	2 parrots	3 tigers	4 lions	5 leopards
6 penguins	7 pandas	8 rhinos	9 zebras	10 snakes

2 Look, read, and write.

1 They're long.
They're _snakes._

2 They're fast.
They're _____.

3 They're black and orange.
They're _____.

4 They're big and scary.
They're _____.

5 They're funny.
They're _____.

6 They're strong.
They're _____.

Tell me!
*They're black
and white.
They're cute.*

40

Extra time? Which animals have four legs?

5.06 Listen and check (✓). Then write.

1

a

b

2

a

b

They _____can_____ swim.

They _____can't_____ walk.

They're _____ .

They _____ walk.

They _____ fly.

They're _____ .

2 **Look and write.**

1 _____Can_____ they walk?

Yes, they _____can._____

2 _____ they fly?

No, _____ .

3 _____ they run?

_____

4 _____ sing?

_____

I can shine!

3 **Write about your favorite animals.**

My favorite animals are _____ .

They can _____ .

They can't _____ .

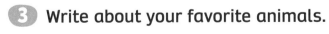

Extra time? What animals start with *p* and *l*?

1 **Look and circle. Then write.**

1 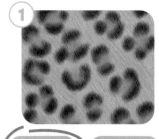 **2**  **3**  **4**

(spots) stripes   fur   feathers   spots   stripes   tail   wings

spots

2 [SB p56–57] **Read and check (✓) for long-eared jerboas.**

a *They have fur and spots.*
They can run fast. ☐

b *They have long tails and big ears.*
They can jump very high. ☐

c *They have wings and feathers.*
They can fly. ☐

Let's imagine!

What do you think?
The story is: OK ☆ *good* ☆☆
great ☆☆☆

I can shine! ✳

3 **Choose an animal from the story. Write.**

They're _____ .
They have _____ .
They can _____ .
They can't _____ .

Extra time? What animals in the story are cute/big/scary/strong?

1 **Look, read, and circle. Then write.**

1 They **have / don't have** spots. Do they have stripes? Yes, _they do._

2 They **have / don't have** legs. _____ they _____ a tail? No, _____.

3 They _____ wings. Do _____ feathers?
_____

4 _____ fur. _____ stripes?
_____

2 **Read and match.**

Let's build!
Say what the animals have or don't have.

1 Let's learn about pandas.

2 Let's watch a movie.

3 Let's look on the internet.

a Yes, that sounds great!

b I'm not sure. I don't like movies.

c Sure! I like pandas.

I can shine!

3 **Think and write. Then ask and answer.**

Let's learn about _____.

Yes, _____.

Do they have _____ ?

Yes, _____.

Do they have _____ ?

No, _____.

Pronunciation Find and circle the one that doesn't belong: snake   sure   spots   stripes

1 **Read and circle.**

1 It's very hot in the **ocean** / **grassland.**

2 There's a lot of fruit in the **desert** / **jungle.**

3 There isn't a lot of water in the **desert** / **ocean.**

4 It's cold in the **jungle** / **ocean.**

2 🎧 5.16 **Listen and match. Then write.**

1  2  3  4

a desert b jungle c ocean d grassland

1 Penguins live in the _____ ocean. _____

2 Some snakes live in the _____.

3 Parrots and _____ live in the _____.

4 Rhinos and _____ live in _____.

3 **Choose an animal. Write.**

Leopards live in the jungle. _____

_____

Can you find out where pandas live?

Extra time? Penguins have wings but they can't fly. True or false?

1 Read and check (✓). Then write.

My fact sheet puzzle, by Tessa

They live in grassland.

They have a tail and they have four legs.

They don't have fur and they don't have feathers.

They can walk, run, and swim.

They can't fly and they can't jump.

They're _____ .

2 Give it a go **Plan your fact sheet puzzle.**

1 Where do they live? _____

2 What do they have? _____, _____

3 What can they do? _____, _____

4 What are they? _____

I can **shine!**

3 Write your fact sheet puzzle.

My fact sheet puzzle, by _____

_____

_____

_____

_____

_____

Check your work! Remember! They don't have   They can't

1 Write the words.

Down

Across

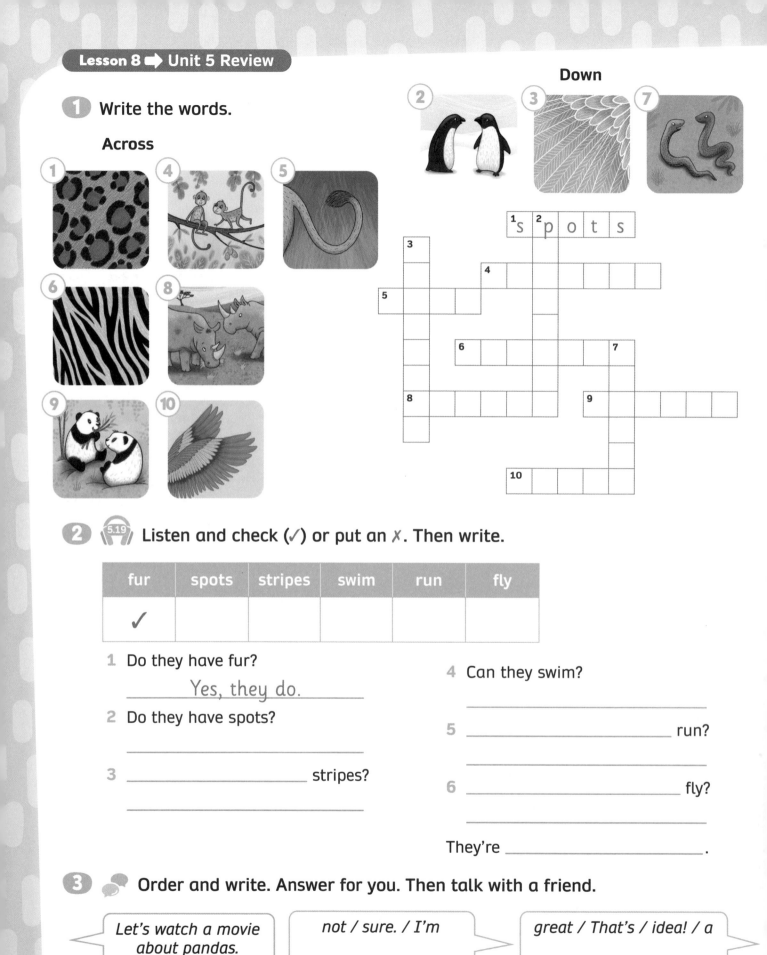

2 Listen and check (✓) or put an ✗. Then write.

fur	spots	stripes	swim	run	fly
✓					

1 Do they have fur?

__Yes, they do.__

2 Do they have spots?

_____

3 _____ stripes?

_____

4 Can they swim?

_____

5 _____ run?

_____

6 _____ fly?

_____

They're _____.

3 Order and write. Answer for you. Then talk with a friend.

Let's watch a movie about pandas.

not / sure. / I'm

_____

great / That's / idea! / a

_____

Extra time? They have [g i n w s] and [e f a h t r e s]. They're... .

1 💬 **Think and complete. Then talk with a friend.**

| tigers | snakes | penguins | monkeys | parrots | leopards | fish |

	They have feathers.	They don't have feathers.
ocean		
jungle		

2 **Make your lapbook. Find pictures or draw. Then write.**

My favorite animal habitat

1 What's your favorite habitat? _____

2 What animals live there? _____

3 What do they have? _____

4 What can they do? _____

Grassland

Lions live in grassland.
They have a long
tail and fur.
They can run.

Zebras live in grassland, too.
They have stripes and fur.
They can swim.

Home-school link 🔗 Tell your family about your favorite animal habitat.

47

6 Come on an adventure!

Let's review! SB p54–55

Think and write.

What animals have fur?

_____ _____

_____ _____

Lesson 1 ➡ Vocabulary

1 Read and number.

1 skateboarding	2 rock-climbing	3 riding a bike	4 fishing
5 reading a map	6 building a fort	7 sailing	8 drawing
9 having a picnic	10 hiking a nature trail		

2 Look, read, and write.

1 I'm <u>having a picnic.</u> I have cheese and tomato sandwiches.

2 I'm _____ a picture of the park.

3 I'm _____. I'm lost!

4 I'm not _____,
I'm _____ to my
friend's house.

5 I'm not _____,
I'm _____
on the lake.

Tell me!
*What activities
are you good at?*

Extra time? What activities can you do at the beach?

1   Listen and circle.

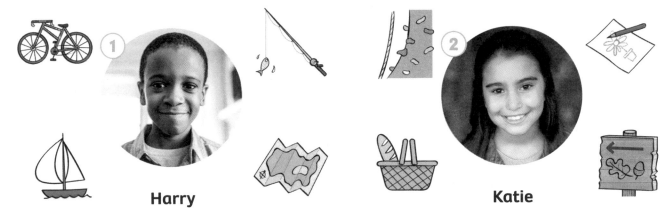

Harry   Katie

2 Look at Activity 1. Then write.

| fishing ~~riding a bike~~ |
| sailing   reading a map |

| rock-climbing   having a picnic |
| hiking a nature trail   drawing |

1 Harry <u>isn't riding a bike.</u>

He _____ .

_____

He's _____ .

2 Katie _____ .

She _____ .

_____

_____

I can shine!

3 Look and write. Then tell a friend.

She isn't _____ .

She's _____ .

_____

_____

Extra time? Which new word is easy for you? Which is difficult for you?

1 **Look and write.**

| lake mountain river island ~~forest~~ country |

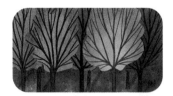

1 ___forest___   2 _____   3 _____

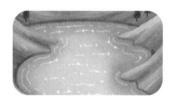

4 _____   5 _____   6 _____

2 SB p66–67 ➡ **Read and number. Then write.** | great reading doing library lake |

a   **b** 1   **c**   **d**

The _____ is behind these trees. Follow me!

He's _____ the map.

Wow! What a _____ adventure!

I can see the _____ and the country. What's that man _____?

I can shine!

3 **Write for you.**

1 I think the adventure trail is _____.

   (fun) (scary) (exciting)

2 When it's raining, I like _____.

   (being outside) (staying at home) (having a picnic)

Extra time? How do the children help Thomas in the story?

1 **Look and write.**

1 What_'s_ she _doing?_
She's _____.

2 _____ he _____?
_____

3 _Is_ he _riding a bike?_
No, _he isn't._
_____ he _____?
Yes, _____.

4 _____ she _____?
No, _____.
_____ she _____?
Yes, _____.

2 **Order and write. Then number.**

> country. / the / go / Let's / to

_____ ☐

> today? / like / weather / What's / the

_____ ☐

Let's build!
Choose a picture in Activity 1.
Ask and answer to guess which one.

> 's / sunny. / It

_____ ☐

I can shine! ✦

3 💬 **Think and write. Then ask and answer.**

> What's _____ in the winter?

> It's _____.

> Let's _____.

Pronunciation Find and circle the one that doesn't belong: snow   show   shower   know

1 **Read and match.**

a

a It's windy. She's windsurfing on the lake.

b She's kayaking on the lake. It's a cool sport!

c He's in the mountains and he's skiing. He's having fun!

d She's sledding in the snow. It's scary, but it's exciting.

Do you prefer summer or winter activities? Why?

2 6.16 **Listen and write.**

1 **Summer**

_____
_____
_____
_____

2 **Winter**

_____
_____
_____
_____

3 **Write for you.**

I like sledding in the mountains in the winter.

I like _____ in the winter.

I like _____ in the summer.

Extra time? Can you go skiing when it isn't snowy?

1 Read and check (✓).

BLOG

Home   About   Blog

Home > Blog > Family trip

My family trip to the lake
by Tatiana

I'm with my family. We're on a trip to
a beautiful lake.
There's an island in the lake.
We're having a lot of fun!
This is me! I'm sailing on the lake.
My brother is windsurfing.
My sister is riding a bike by the lake.

2 Give it a go **Plan your blog post.**

1 Where's your family trip? _____

2 Who's with you? _____

3 What activities are you doing? _____

4 What activities are your family doing? _____

I can shine!

3 Write your blog post.

BLOG

Home   About   Blog

My family trip to _____ , **by** _____

_____

_____

_____

_____

_____

Check your work! Check your spelling. have ⇨ having hike ⇨ hiking

1 **Find and circle. Then write.**

A	R	H	A	V	I	N	G	Q	C
M	E	R	H	B	C	W	Q	A	L
O	A	I	S	L	A	K	E	B	I
U	D	V	L	K	Q	P	D	N	M
N	I	E	H	I	K	I	N	G	B
T	N	R	Y	M	W	D	G	K	I
A	G	R	I	D	I	N	G	G	N
I	D	R	A	W	I	N	G	P	G
N	W	X	Z	W	R	N	R	T	Y
S	C	B	U	I	L	D	I	N	G

1 He's <u>building</u> a fort.

2 She's skiing in the _____.

3 He isn't _____ a nature trail.

4 She's _____ a picnic.

5 Is he _____ a map?

6 Is she sailing on the _____?

7 He isn't rock- _____.

8 She likes _____ pictures.

9 Is she _____ her bike?

10 She's fishing next to the _____.

2 **6.19** **Write. Then listen and check.**

1 He's in the ___country.___

_____ skateboarding?

No, _____.

He's _____.

2 She's next to the _____.

_____ fishing?

No, _____.

_____

3 💬 **Write and answer for you. Then talk with a friend.**

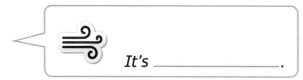

It's _____.

Let's go _____.

Extra time? You can do this with paper. You need a pencil.

1 💬 **Think and complete. Then talk with a friend.**

Choose two places close to your home. What can you do there?

| park   town square   beach   country   river   mountains |

Place	Summer activity	Winter activity

2 **Make your lapbook. Find pictures or draw. Then write.**

A place I like to visit

1 Choose a place from Activity 1. _____

2 What activities can you do there? _____

3 Who do you go with? _____

4 Can you go there in summer or winter? _____

5 What's the weather like? _____

Home-school link 📱 Tell your family about a place you like to visit.

55

1 Read and write.

BLOG

Home   About   **Blog**   ⋮

Kate Hall's nature trips

Kate is in the ¹[t a i m o n u n s] <u>mountains.</u>

She's ²[c o r k   g i n c i l b m]

_____ – _____.

She isn't ³[g w a n r i d] _____.

There are some ⁴[s p a d r e o l] _____.

They can't ⁵[f y l] _____ but they

⁶[n c a] _____ run.

They have ⁷[s t o p s] _____.

They don't have ⁸[p e r s t i s] _____.

2 🎧 6.22 Look, read, and circle. Listen and check. Then ask and answer.

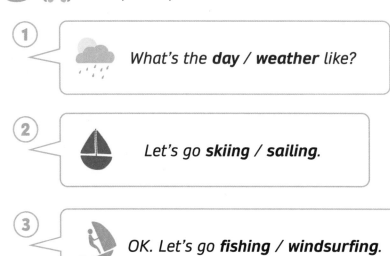

① What's the **day / weather** like?

It's **snowy / windy**.

② Let's go **skiing / sailing**.

✗ **Yes, sure! / I'm not sure.**

③ OK. Let's go **fishing / windsurfing**.

✓ That's a **great / bad** idea!

3 Read and write.

1 ___Do___ the parrots have fur?
___No, they don't.___

2 _____ they _____ feathers?

_____

3 ___Can___ they swim?

_____

4 _____ fly?

_____

5 ___Is___ the boy having a picnic?

_____

6 ___ he _____ a nature trail?

_____

Mini-project

4 Imagine and write.

BLOG

Blog ⋮

Kate is in _____.

She's _____.

She isn't _____.

There are _____.

They can _____.

They have _____.

_____.

Time to **shine!**

5 Read and check (✓). Tell your friend.

1 I can write a fact file about an animal. ☐

2 I can write a blog post about a school trip. ☐

3 I can talk about what animals have and don't have. ☐

4 I can ask and answer about what friends are doing. ☐

My favorite song is in
Unit 5 ☐ Unit 6 ☐

My favorite story is in
Unit 5 ☐ Unit 6 ☐

6 Vote. Sing or role-play.

Review 3 **57**

 **from Rise and Shine Library**

1 **Think and write.**

> history   monkeys   sailing   sports center   geography
> storyteller   reading corner   snakes   movie theater   fishing

At school	In town	In the library	In the jungle	At the lake
_____	_____	_____	_____	_____
_____	_____	_____	_____	_____

2  **Listen and number. Then write.**

a  [1]

They have ____fur.____

They can _____ high.

b

Lena is _____ for animals.

Daniel isn't _____ a fort.

c

Rafa isn't very good at _____.

Does Lena like helping people?

_____

d

There _____ a movie theater.

Are there any police officers?

_____

3 **Look at Activity 2. Ask and answer.**

> *Do the jerboas have fur?*

> *Does Lena like doing crafts?*

> *What's Daniel doing?*

> *Are there any stores in the town square?*

4 Read and match.

a He likes drawing. He's good at painting. He doesn't like playing sports.

b She likes being outdoors. She loves animals. Her favorite school subject is science.

c He's good at sports. He can run fast. His favorite subjects are P.E. and math.

d She likes taking pictures and using computers. She's kind and smart.

5 Make your lapbook. Find pictures or draw. Then write.

My favorite things about Rise and Shine Library

1 My favorite character in Rise and Shine Library is _____.

2 I like _____ because _____.

3 My favorite new words are _____.

4 My favorite story is about _____.

5 I like the song from Unit _____.

6 My favorite fun fact is _____.

Home-school link Tell your family about Rise and Shine Library.

World Teachers' Day

1 Look and write.

music room
computer lab
gym
classroom
~~cafeteria~~
science lab

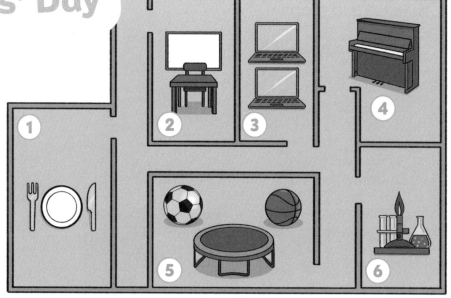

1 _cafeteria_
2 _____
3 _____
4 _____
5 _____
6 _____

2 (8.04) Listen, order, and write.

teachers / our / for

Hooray _____!

and / kind / help / they / us

They're _____.

World Kindness Day

3 Look and write.

care   give   ~~help~~
thank you   smile   talk

4 (8.08) Listen and circle.

It's World **Kindness /**

Helping Day!

Let's be **care / kind**,

Let's all **play / talk**.

1 _help_ someone

2 _____ someone a gift

3 _____ to a friend

4 say _____

5 _____

6 _____ about someone

World Book Day

5 Find and circle. Then write.

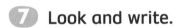

tellastory inventorkingqueencostumedressup

6 🎧 **8.12** Listen, order, and write.

dress up / Book Day / for / World

Let's _____

_____ !

hip-hip-hooray / choose /
a / costume –

Let's _____

_____ !

1 _____

2 _____

3 _____

4 tell a story

5 _____

6 _____

World Environment Day

7 Look and write.

> turn off   vegetables
> plant   walk
> ~~recycle~~   water

8 🎧 **8.16** Listen and match.

1 We can help   a to school.

2 We can grow   b off lights.

3 We can walk   c the planet.

4 We can turn   d vegetables.

1 recycle

2 grow _____

3 _____
to school

4 _____
trees

5 _____
the plants

6 _____
lights

Word connections

Word connections key

Places

People

Activities

Describing words

Welcome

Write your own new words!

Places in the library
courtyard
gallery
information desk
multimedia room
reading corner
study area

Library objects
beanbag
computer
poster
TV

1 All about school!

School subjects
art
drama
English
geography
history
math
music
P.E.
science
technology

Routine actions
brush my teeth
go to bed
go to school
have breakfast
take a shower
wake up

2 Explore our town!

Places in town

bus stop	theater
cafe	police station
drugstore	sports center
grocery store	store
hospital	town square
movie	

What other places do you know?

Jobs

bus driver
doctor
librarian
police officer
sales clerk
server

3 Let's tell stories!

Book characters

astronaut	princess
explorer	spy
inventor	storyteller
pirate	superhero
prince	villain

What other people do you know?

Adjectives

brave
cute
kind
scary
smart
strong

4 Party at the library!

Hobbies

acting	painting
coding	playing chess
having a party	playing video games
juggling	taking pictures
learning an instrument	trading cards

Activities

being outside
doing crafts
helping people
learning something new
playing sports
using computers

5 Let's save our animals!

Animals

leopards	penguins
lions	rhinos
monkeys	snakes
pandas	tigers
parrots	zebras

Animal parts

feathers	stripes
fur	tail
spots	wings

What other describing words do you know?

6 Come on an adventure!

Outdoor activities

building a fort
drawing
fishing
having a picnic
hiking a nature trail
reading a map
riding a bike
rock-climbing
sailing
skateboarding

What other activities do you know?

Places in nature

country
forest
island
lake
mountain
river

What other places do you know?